Developing Pupils' Social Communication Skills

Practical Resources

**Penny Barratt, Julie Border, Helen Joy,
Alison Parkinson, Mo Potter and George Thomas**

David Fulton Publishers
London

Leicester City Council LEA
Leicestershire County Council LEA
Leicestershire and Rutland Healthcare NHS Trust

David Fulton Publishers Ltd
The Chiswick Centre, 414 Chiswick High Road, London W4 5TF

www.fultonpublishers.co.uk

First published in Great Britain by David Fulton Publishers 2000
Reprinted 2002 (twice)

Note: The right of the authors to be identified as the authors of this work has been asserted by them in accordance with the Copyright, Designs and Patents Act 1988.

British Library Cataloguing in Publication Data
A catalogue record for this book is available from the British Library.

ISBN 1–85346–728–6

Typeset by Mark Heslington, Scarborough, North Yorkshire
Printed in Great Britain by Bell and Bain Ltd., Glasgow

Contents

Acknowledgements and Author Details

The writers would like to thank all the people who have made this book possible, either by suggesting games or trialling them in schools or nurseries. Those who merit special mention are Christine Reeve, Leicester Education Authority, Emma Kehoe, Leicestershire Education Authority and Sara Hoy, Leicestershire and Rutland Healthcare Trust.

Special thanks to Val Painter, Margaret Harrison and Jan Phillips for their secretarial support.

The authors

Alison Parkinson
Julie Border
Speech and Language Therapy
    Department
Leicestershire and Rutland
    Healthcare NHS Trust
Leicestershire

George Thomas
Learning and Autism Support Team
Special Needs Teaching Service
Leicester City Council LEA

Penny Barratt
Leicestershire County Council LEA
Menphys Centre
Leicester

Helen Joy
Mo Potter
Autism Outreach Team
Specialist Teaching Service
Leicestershire County Council LEA

1 Introduction

Learning to communicate with other people is arguably the most important learning that children do. The process starts early. Language emerges from looks and glances, hand waving, smiles, and noises exchanged between parent and child.

For most children, learning to relate to other people comes naturally. They will have different styles, with some learning more quickly than others, but, broadly speaking, they all learn in the same way. They learn where to look, and what to expect, how to copy and how to affect what another person does. They learn to share information, ideas and feelings, moving from the close circle of the family towards confident independence in the wider world.

In order to learn to communicate, young children need the means to do so. They also need opportunities and reasons. There are many means or ways of communicating, for example, speech, facial expressions, body language, signing and gesture. Opportunities to communicate are equally varied, but in every situation children will need an attentive listener who responds to them. Children develop many reasons to communicate. They make requests, they ask questions and give information; they express their feelings and generally enjoy talking to other people.

Children with social communication problems by definition often have trouble picking up ways of interacting and communicating with their peers. As teachers, we have to work on the development of children's communication in order to help them bridge the gap between themselves and other people. So much of their future happiness and learning depends on being able to join in and to understand what others expect of them.

Children learn through playing with adults and other children. Play helps intellectual, emotional and physical development and provides a context for learning social skills. This book uses traditional children's games to develop children's communication. Many of the games outlined here have 'been about for years' and countless numbers of children have enjoyed playing them. As they play, they practise approaching, communicating and cooperating with others. The games here are being used to provide a structured approach to developing and enhancing children's communication skills. They can also be a lot of fun.

This book is for all school staff. It may be used by class teachers to provide ideas for some whole class games that can promote the development of communication. It is, however, probably best used by classroom assistants or teachers who work with smaller groups of children.

You will need to complete the assessment on pages 7 and 8 for each child with social communication difficulties. Once this task has been undertaken you can plan your activities using the monthly and daily planning sheets. It is important to include activities that emphasise the strengths of the child with social communication difficulties in the sessions, as well as addressing their weaknesses.

A different game is described on each page. Many of these games will be familiar to you and the children for whom they are intended. The aim is to promote communication through familiar children's games. Some of the games suggested are for playing outside, some in the school hall, some on a carpet area and others around a table. Different games may require a different number of players. A logo in the top right hand corner of each page will help you to see at a glance where the game is intended to be played and how many players are required (see table below).

Logo – Explanatory table	
	Indicates a game to be played with up to 10 players around a table.
	Indicates a game to be played with up to 10 players in a small indoor space.
	Indicates a game to be played inside or outside with 10+ players.

The activities are organised throughout the book by the key skill that they address. This is shown in the top left hand corner. Below that is a cross reference to other skills that the activity may help to develop.

Important information is given at the bottom of the sheet about the role of the adult and the prompts he or she can use to promote the development of communication. This is the difference between simply teaching children how to play the games and using the games as a vehicle to develop communication skills.

Think carefully about the children who will make up the group. The authors would strongly suggest that as well as children with social communication difficulties ideally developing peers should be included as well. Try to use friendships as this will increase the likelihood of the games and skills being generalised and taken up at other times without adult intervention. This book contains a host of information about group organisation and how to steer the sessions toward tangible results.

We believe that communication should be natural and fun for all children and their helpers too!

2 Assessment

Communication is so much at the heart of everything that we do together that it can be very difficult to stand back and look at it objectively. We may be charmed, irritated or unmoved by another person's behaviour towards us, but we seldom try to analyse how they have this effect upon us. We are too emotionally bound up in the whole process ourselves to look at the mechanism.

When we do start to look at how we communicate with one another we realise that there is no simple pattern. Instead, we are presented with a human process that is constantly changing, weaving and adapting to need, circumstance, situation and intention. The assessment sheets given here attempt to pick out some of the threads of this process so that we can begin to identify areas where we can support the development of children with social communication difficulties. We have called these threads key skills, which are directly addressed in the games, and other skills, which are referred to throughout the collection.

Fifteen key skills are identified in the assessment and the games that follow.

Eight are non-verbal
- I can share a focus of attention
- I can demonstrate listening and looking skills
- I can attract someone's attention
- I can understand and use facial expression
- I can understand and use gesture and body posture
- I can play a role/pretend
- I can show awareness of others
- I can listen and do

Seven are verbal
- I can say what I want and don't want
- I can start and finish talking to other people
- I can maintain a topic
- I can give and receive information
- I can say what I like and don't like
- I can alter my style
- I can apologise

The next two pages contain descriptions and explanations of these key skills.

On pages seven and eight are two assessment grids to fill in for each child with social communication difficulties. This section finishes with a glossary of eight other skills referred to in the activities.

In order to determine the child's strengths and weaknesses in each area, someone familiar with the child will need to carry out the assessment. This will involve:

1. Setting a time-frame over which the assessment will be completed, maybe as long as half a term.
2. Familiarising yourself with the key skills to establish a framework for observation.
3. Observing the child communicating in as wide a range of settings as possible. Watch him or her in the classroom, at playtime, on a school trip and with different people, such as teachers, school staff, peers and parents.

You may need to set up situations in order to give opportunities to elicit some of these skills, for example, giving the child a task without all the necessary equipment may lead to him or her attracting someone's attention. This is essential if you do not see a particular skill in your general observations.

4. Discussing your findings with someone else who knows the child.
5. Making a judgement about the behaviours you observe, analysing them according to the grid and rating them using the scale. The rating scale takes into account frequency and appropriateness.

Typical behaviour in the context in which the observations have been carried out is represented by point three on the rating scale. If the focus child shows the same behaviours as other children he or she scores three for the relevant key skills. If you sometimes see the child using a key skill but not to the same extent as his or her peers, then score two. Points one and four on the scale represent ineffective use of the key skills. This may be because they are not used at all, score one, or occur excessively or inappropriately, score four. Only expressive skills can be overused. Receptive skills cannot be described in this way. If misunderstandings in any key skill do occur they should be scored four as being inappropriate.

6. Evaluating the child's progress in acquiring the key skills will involve repeating the assessment after using the games for a designated period of time. Refer to the planning section for advice.

Once the assessment is completed you can use the guidance provided to plan your sessions. (See pages 12–16)

Key skills

The following paragraphs are intended to guide observations of the focus child by giving an outline of various aspects of communicative behaviour. Each skill relates directly to the assessment sheet.

Non-verbal skills

I can share a focus of attention
People engage in the same moment, activity, or event, which involves looking and listening together, sharing looks, enjoyment and meaning.

I can demonstrate listening and looking skills
People share looks when they are speaking and listening. Speaking and listening without looking can appear rude. Looking helps people know that you are interested.

I can attract someone's attention
All conversations begin with one person attracting another's attention in a way which fits in with the situation; from shouting 'hello' to gently tapping someone's shoulder or putting up a hand in the classroom.

I can understand and use facial expression
Making sense of people's faces is as important as understanding what they say. Likewise, people understand what others mean by their facial expressions. Facial expressions can complement or even give the lie to people's words. They can also be overdone.

I can understand and use gesture and body posture
Gestures and body posture are used naturally to emphasise what people mean. They can go along with verbal language or stand alone. Some, such as pointing, have specific meanings; others simply regulate the 'to and fro' of conversation.

I can play a role/pretend
Pretending helps people to try out new ways of behaving and to understand other's behaviours. It gives an opportunity to practise how it might feel to be in different social situations.

I can show awareness of others
This means comparing and recognising how other people look and behave.

I can listen and do
This involves listening and then acting upon the information heard. It requires children understanding and processing the language they hear and acting upon it.

Verbal skills

I can say what I want and don't want

In everyday life there are thousands of choices to be made; people need to be able to ask for what they need and want and to reject things they do not want in ways which fit the situation. It is one of the most important reasons for communicating.

I can start and finish talking to other people

When talking to other people we need to be able to get their attention either non-verbally (as described above – attracting someone's attention) or by using spoken language, e.g. calling someone. Conversations have natural beginnings and ends, although the latter can be subtler than the former, e.g. by tone of voice. Effective communicators are able to recognise and react to the things others say and do to begin and end conversations.

I can maintain a topic

Every conversation is about something. People tend to stay on the topic introduced by the first speaker until it reaches a natural end. Everybody keeps to the point, but topics can change during a conversation. The effective communicator can adapt to this change. He or she can also recognise when a conversation has gone wrong and have the skills to put it right.

I can give and receive information

Within school a lot of communication is about giving and receiving information. This helps children learn about the world. It involves listening as well as speaking skills.

I can say what I like and don't like

People say how they feel, give their opinion, agree and disagree, give compliments and criticism and accept other people doing likewise. These are the fundamentals of assertiveness.

I can alter my style

Style includes intonation, speed of speaking and tone and volume of voice. People are able to change these to fit the situation, e.g. children will use a more formal style when talking to the head teacher or a 'playground style' with their peers.

I can apologise

This involves recognising that something is wrong, knowing that it needs to be acknowledged and then having the right words or skills to do so.

Assessment Sheet				
Non-Verbal Skills				
List of Skills	1	2	3	4
I can share a focus of attention				
I can demonstrate listening and looking skills				
I can attract someone's attention				
I can understand and use facial expression				
I can understand and use gesture and body posture				
I can play a role/pretend				
I can show awareness of others				
I can listen and do				

Key

1 Never   **3** Appropriately

2 Sometimes   **4** Excessively or Inappropriately

Name _____   **Date** _____

Assessor _____

Reassessment date _____

Assessor _____

Assessment Sheet				
Verbal Skills				
List of Skills	1	2	3	4
I can say what I want and don't want				
I can start and finish talking to other people				
I can maintain a topic				
I can give and receive information				
I can say what I like and don't like				
I can alter my style				
I can apologise				

Key	
1 Never	**3** Appropriately
2 Sometimes	**4** Excessively or Inappropriately

Name _____ **Date** _____

Assessor _____

Reassessment date _____

Assessor _____

Other skills

Some social communication skills are so pervasive that they are involved in many of the games in this book. They are listed separately here, so they can be identified when using the planning sheets. This is not meant to imply that they are any less important than the skills identified in the assessment, more that they run alongside and complement the identified assessment skills.

I can take turns
Turn-taking is an important communication skill. At its simplest it means taking turns formally in a board game for instance or, at a more complex level, the taking of turns in conversation. This involves being aware of when to take your turn by anticipating pauses and reading the body language of the person you are talking to. It involves listening carefully to what the person has to say so that you can maintain the topic of conversation. Asking and answering questions is a way of turn taking.

I can win or lose
Many young children find it hard to win or lose 'gracefully', and those with social communication difficulties may find competitive games particularly difficult. This book offers a range of games, some involving winning and losing, some not. It may be useful to point out which is which to some children and to 'set up' some games so that everyone gets a chance to win. Accepting that you have lost involves being able to take the game lightly and focusing on the fun element. Enjoying winning involves being able to empathise with the losers.

I can remember important things about other people
Memory is an important component of language processing, but this aspect is not the focus here. A 'social memory' involves remembering important social information about others, such as what makes them happy or sad, what hobbies they have, food or music they like or when their birthday is.

I can tolerate proximity
Keeping the appropriate social distance from others, depending on familiarity, is an important social communication skill. If people invade other's 'personal space' it can feel uncomfortable, as can staying too far away.

I can choose
Making choices involves knowing what there is to choose between, deciding what you want and communicating your choice in a socially appropriate way.

I can ask for help and clarification
Asking for help can involve many different communicative styles depending on the problem at hand, e.g. shouting out when you are in pain or putting up your hand when you need help in class. Asking for clarification is a much more subtle skill. It involves being aware of when you have misunderstood and knowing how to ask someone to rephrase or explain.

I can anticipate

This skill requires awareness of the intentions and behaviour of other people. This understanding is built up over time so that we are able to anticipate how another person may behave. It involves remembering how others have behaved in the past so we can predict how they may behave in the future.

I can take the lead and follow others

Within social situations, including conversation, somebody usually takes the lead, such as deciding what to do next, introducing a new idea to talk about and getting other people involved. The leader can change quickly depending on the situation. In school, the person taking the lead is normally the teacher but he or she can choose to pass this role to someone else, either by nominating someone or by seeking volunteers. Any child taking on the role of leader may need coaching, and equally those children following this lead may need support in recognising the shift in responsibility.

3 Planning

Completing the assessment sheets

It is a good idea for more than one person to fill in the assessment sheets. Doing this allows you to check whether how you see the child is the same as other people. It also gives you information about the skills the child has in different settings, for example, at home as well as at school.

Photocopy the two assessment sheets, one for non-verbal skills and one for verbal skills. Ask two or three people to complete this. You may need to discuss jointly what you mean by the terms 'never', 'sometimes', 'appropriately' etc. before you start. The people who should fill in this assessment are those who know the child best. This would usually include the parent(s), class teacher and classroom support assistant. A speech and language therapist is likely to be particularly astute when looking for these aspects of communication, if one is involved.

Where to start

Once the assessment sheets have been completed compile a list of the areas with which the child has particular difficulty, areas where he or she does well and a list of the areas that fall in between. It might help to use the pro forma below:

Good aspects of social communication
Poor aspects of social communication
Emerging aspects of social communication

Once you have collated the assessment information you can plan your sessions using the following guidance.

Long-term planning

Before you can start planning your sessions you will need to know the group of children you will be working with. As mentioned earlier, the authors feel that it is really useful for the child with social communication difficulties to work alongside children who do not have such difficulties so that they can act as role models. However, as we have all worked in schools, we realise that this is not always possible and that often you may work with a group of children who all have similar difficulties.

If you are working with a group of children where only one child has specific difficulties then your planning for the sessions will relate directly to their assessment. However, if you are working with a group of children who all have social communication difficulties you will need to take into account all of their assessments when planning the sessions. If only one child has difficulties with one area it is still valid to include work on this in the sessions, but you need to balance this across the group of children.

Whatever the make-up of the group, it is important to choose activities that will succeed as well as those that will be more difficult. We recognise that you will need to choose activities that you can easily use so refer to the logo at the top right hand corner of the page for a quick indication of location and numbers.

Example

It is also important to plan for half a term of sessions so that you know what you will be doing next. Ask yourself the following questions:

- What is this child or group good at?
- What are this child's or group's emerging skills?
- What are the areas the child or group finds most difficult?

You will need to consider:

- The things the children like to do.
- The facilities and resources that you have at your disposal.
- Which games the children will succeed and do well at and which they will find more difficult.

You will need to think quite carefully about how often you will be running this session (we would suggest a minimum of once a week) and for how long the session will last, as this will influence your planning. Knowing your group, you will also need to estimate how long an activity will last. It is important to repeat games and activities so that skills can be practised within a familiar routine, but the children should not become bored with the repetition. This, too, needs careful consideration.

Complete the following form after thinking about the above.

Spread the activities over the weeks of the half term and include them on the following page. Remember the need for repetition – children like to repeat games they have enjoyed.

Be prepared to alter your planning when the group has started. Some skills may be acquired quickly. Others may take longer, or be too difficult at first. As the games differ in length and complexity there are no hard and fast rules as to how many you play in a session. It may be useful to always start and end with a familiar, quick game to mark out the structure of the session.

In the next half term I want to introduce the following games/activities:
To extend and encourage areas of strength
To extend and encourage emerging skills
To develop particular areas of difficulty with social communication

Name(s)..

Date..

	Activities	Observations and Comments
Week 1 Warm-up Activity 1 Activity 2 Closing		
Week 2 Warm-up Activity 1 Activity 2 Closing		
Week 3 Warm-up Activity 1 Activity 2 Closing		
Week 4 Warm-up Activity 1 Activity 2 Closing		
Week 5 Warm-up Activity 1 Activity 2 Closing		
Week 6 Warm-up Activity 1 Activity 2 Closing		

After each session ask yourself these questions for each child:

- How did he or she do in relation to the areas I was trying to address?
- Is there anything particular I need to note for future sessions (e.g. did he or she particularly like or dislike something?)
- What do I need to take into account for the next session?

Assessment needs to be ongoing and to inform your planning. You may wish to record interesting aspects of the performance of the focus child or group in the box for observations and comments. Photocopy this sheet as you wish. You may like to do a fuller re-assessment using the model supplied in the book, possibly at termly intervals.

Planning the sessions

About the group: Careful thought has to be given when choosing a group of children to work with the focus child. The group you select is likely to have an effect on how the activity goes. It is important to think about the friendships in the class and to include children who do not have any particular speech, language or learning difficulties. Although friendship is one of the factors to bear in mind when choosing a group, it is not the only one. Other children in the class may benefit from this work, either directly, in that they too have speech and language needs; or indirectly, in that they are isolated socially, under-confident or need to broaden their social use of language. It will be important to choose some children who are able, but patient and willing to give time as others learn. Their role will be to encourage, act as an example and keep the pace of the game going. It may be a good idea to change the group depending on the activity that is being undertaken. You do not have to stay with the same group of children each time, although there is some benefit in setting up a core with whom the focus child can identify.

Friendships: It is important to take friendships into account for a number of reasons. Firstly, we need to ensure that children participate willingly and in a relaxed atmosphere. We have an insight into the value of these games as 'work', but it is important to remember that games should, first and foremost, be fun. Secondly, they are important because we hope that the children will want to use the games in their own time. Children with social and communication difficulties often have trouble fitting in at playtime. They may be unaware of the opportunities to play with other children or they may find the whole experience too noisy and frightening. When the focus child has something familiar and enjoyable to do in the playground there is much more chance of the skills being used in a natural manner.

Size: Remember that the group will have to run smoothly even though some of the participants may have difficulty. Group size will be an important factor. For example, if a pupil has difficulty taking turns it would be unwise to make the group too large for a game that required turn taking. There are guidelines as to group size with each game described.

Status: If the children see taking part in work of this type as something special there will be a knock-on effect of increasing the status of the focus child in the eyes of the rest of his or her peer group.

Timing: Try to run the group at regular times. You will probably need 30–45 minutes for each session.

Putting it into practice

Organisation: Make sure that the game starts with an introduction of what is going to happen. It is a good idea to start and finish with a quiet meeting so that the aims and rules of the game can be discussed and reviewed, and any learning recapped. Use this meeting time to explain what is being looked at. Be explicit because many pupils with social and communication difficulties may not realise what it is they are doing. Keep to this routine so that the game sessions have a clear beginning and end. Some of the games will be boisterous. The children will need an opportunity to calm down before they return to more formal work. Use clear 'starts' and 'finishes'. Timers, clocks and music cues all provide a definite structure.

Roles: Try not to talk too much, especially when the game gets underway. Some of the games will need you to take part as a leader, while in others you may be one of the players. It can be difficult to be a player and a teacher at the same time. Try not to let the teaching completely overpower the playing. As the children develop skills, try to stand back and let them take the lead.

Let the focus child speak or act for him or herself, although you may need to control the pace of the game so that everyone can have a real turn. If a child needs a lot of support over a long period of playing a game it is likely that the activity is too demanding at the moment. Careful judgements have to be made as to what is possible. Children do not need to fail at play! Seat the focus child beside someone who can act as a 'role model' and/or teacher, quietly providing appropriate verbal and physical prompts.

4 Prompting

Prompting other skills

A number of skills have been identified with which the children may require specific support. You will need to encourage all the children in the group to contribute fully through a series of prompts or cues. Wherever possible choose a prompt that gives the child the minimum amount of support to be successful. The prompts have been organised hierarchically from the highest to the lowest level of support, below.

Taking turns

Children with social and communication difficulties may not understand how to take turns. As many games require the players to take turns we have to be aware of these difficulties. The children are likely to need support in following the game so that they are ready for their turn.

We can use a range of prompts to help children with this, depending on how skilled they are:

1. For those with least social understanding, simply announce 'It's John's turn now.'
2. Others will be able to respond to a direct question, such as 'Whose turn is it now?'
3. The more socially aware may understand the implication behind a loaded remark such as 'We're waiting!'
4. The subtlest prompt (from the point of view of the focus child) would be an exaggerated shrug and a look to encourage others in the group to prompt whose turn will follow.

Some children may be reluctant to hand their turn on to another person, particularly if they are enjoying what they are doing or have a preference for a particular role. This is an important target in itself and will need thoughtful handling.

1. Set the group size so that waiting times are manageable.
2. Reassure the pupil that their turn will come around again and encourage him or her to watch for the turn as it gets closer.

3. Encourage joint attention with remarks such as 'Let's see if Davinder can do it as well as you.'
4. Have a visual sign of whose turn it is. This might be anything from a hat to wear to an object in front of the person.

Listening and looking

Children with social and communication problems may have difficulty being interested in what other people are doing and learning by watching, or listening to, other people. Many of the games in this book provide opportunities for practising this ability and making it relevant. We need to match the prompt that we give to take account of the social understanding of the children.

1. A straightforward verbal instruction, supported by a physical prompt such as a point may suit the needs of the least aware, such as 'Beth, watch (or listen to) Alice.'
2. Sometimes it is preferable not to interrupt the flow of the game with speech. The teacher can tap the person who is not watching and point to who they should be watching.
3. The focus child can be prompted along with the whole group: 'Beth, Chan, Prakash and David; watch (or listen to) Alice.'
4. Some children will have, or be working towards, greater group awareness: 'Everybody watch (or listen to) Alice.'
5. A subtler prompt may be couched as a question: 'Who should we be watching?'
6. Have a visual sign for who is to be watched or listened to, perhaps a shell could be passed as the turn to speak moves around the group. As mentioned above, this sign will also serve as a reminder of whose turn it is.
7. Remind the children of the rules that were discussed at the outset.
8. Avoid repeating instructions by making a 'Look and Listen' card. Hold this up so that the focus child's attention is re-engaged.
9. Show the children appropriate ways of gaining attention. This might mean saying things such as, 'If you want everyone to look at you when we are playing, say "Everyone, look at me."'
10. The teacher or support worker can use non-verbal signs to reinforce their speech. An index finger touching corners of eyes can mean, 'look'. A hand cupped over an ear can mean 'listen' and a finger to the lips 'quiet'. When speaking directly to the focus child, try to avoid idiom or sarcasm. Try to remember his or her literal comprehension.

Part of the reason that some children with social and communication difficulties do not understand the need to watch other people is that they cannot read the subtle messages passed by looks and glances and by body posture. The children may need help with understanding these messages. Some children, particularly those with autistic spectrum disorder, may find it uncomfortable to look other people in the eye.

Pupils may need support, both in giving attention to other people and also with the interpretation of any messages that are not actually spoken, for instance a wink, gesture or facial expression. Use the discussion time before starting the game to outline the social skills needed to play successfully. Depending on which game is to be played, it may be necessary to point out that people pass a lot of messages with their eyes and bodies. It may be useful to role-play different types of body language. Point out the difference between open and relaxed postures and those that are tense and concealing. Some of the games will require you to make clear to the children that they need to pay attention to the eyes, faces and posture of the other players.

Winning and losing

The focus children, particularly those with autistic spectrum disorders, may not accept defeat graciously. This is because they find it hard to predict outcomes and to see things from the point of view of other people. Even when prepared in advance for the possibility of defeat, some children will be unable to believe that it could possibly happen. Others may say that they can handle it, but cannot contain the outrage or disappointment they feel when they actually lose. Predicting consequences and understanding their feelings are very difficult for this group of children.

Managing this problem depends on knowing the children well so that unrealistic aims are not expected of them. Group size and the nature of games chosen will be factors that can be taken into account if you foresee or discover difficulties in this area. Other strategies that may help include:

1. Set clearly expressed and positive targets that are shared by the focus child, his or her parents as well as school staff.
2. Diary records or score sheets of previous games can be used to remind children that they have not always won.
3. At first, avoid games that involve winning and losing if you think this is going to be a difficulty. There are many such games in this book.
4. 'Social stories' can be used to give the focus child guidelines about how to cope with the disappointment of losing. There are many ways of writing a social story but it might look something like this:

On Tuesdays I play games with Mrs Merry, Thomas and Jazdeep.

Sometimes we play games that have a winner.

I like to be the winner very much.

Everybody says 'Well done!' or something like that.

Mrs Merry, Thomas and Jazdeep like to win as well.

I will try to say 'Well done!' when they win.

Everybody will be happy and I might win next time.

---

5. Sometimes it is enough to give the focus child something to do when the feelings start, perhaps counting to ten or having a favourite toy to hold for reassurance.
6. Offer tangible rewards that are significant to the child for keeping cool in the jaws of defeat.

Asking for help and clarification

Children need to learn how to ask for help, including a clarification or repetition of something which has been said to enable them to become independent players, and outside the context of the games, independent communicators. Identifying when communication has broken down is a significant part of this move towards independence. In part this learning can be achieved through the creation of a climate of openness, modelled by the adults within the group.

1. Encourage the children to ask general questions about the games once the rules have been explained.
2. Check that the children have understood by asking them to recap the rules.
3. Occasionally ask, 'Does everyone understand?', 'Did everyone hear that?', etc. and respond very positively to children who say they have not.
4. If a child spontaneously says that they haven't understood, carefully find out which part has caused confusion and reword or revise it. Reward the child for asking for help if you feel this is appropriate.
5. Specifically teach children to ask for help, e.g. Teacher, 'Do you understand that?', Child, 'No', Teacher, 'Ask ___ to explain it, say "explain that again".'

Judging distance

Children may need support either to get closer or to move further apart.

1. Demonstrate the level of proximity needed for any particular game, and act out any inappropriate distances or behaviours for the group to observe and comment on.
2. Use a direct verbal or non-verbal prompt, e.g. gently moving the child to the correct place or asking them to move.
3. Re-state the rules about proximity as the game progresses.
4. An indirect prompt such as 'Where should you be standing?' or 'How close should you be?'

Anticipating

In any of the games the anticipation forms part of each person's turn. Preparing yourself to have your go involves many of the skills involved in listening and looking and turn taking and can be prompted in the same way. You may also need to warn a child specifically that his or her turn is coming up.

Taking the lead and following others

Remember that the children have to take as much charge of the game as possible, especially if they are going to use it in their own time. This means that they need to experience as wide a set of roles as possible. They may need specific advice as to what is required in being the leader, for example, altering the style of the way they say things and what to say when being the prompter.

1. Demonstrate specifically how the person in the leader role behaves and what they say when playing the chosen game. Teach the children the exact phrases to use and other methods of prompting, such as touching someone's arm to get their attention.
2. Reminding the children of the rules on how to be the leader by saying, e.g. 'Can you remember what the leader says?'
3. Prompting the leader to take their role, e.g. by saying 'You're the leader'.
4. An indirect prompt may be something like 'Who's the leader?'

To prompt the children to take their role as followers refer to the sections on turn taking, listening and looking and participation.

Taking part

In order to participate in games in a full and satisfying way children with social and communication difficulties will need a lot of support. We have to think carefully about exactly what we are asking them to do and how we can best help them to a satisfactory outcome.

Most children learn effectively by watching and copying others who are already 'in the know'. Our focus children will benefit from this approach as well, although we will probably have to be a lot more explicit in our guidance. We need to point out the social conventions that others may take for granted, providing an approximate, if somewhat inflexible, formula for the children to follow. This may involve:

1. Using the quiet time before the game starts to work out what this formula will be. Demonstrate to the group how the game will be played. If other children already know the game, use them to demonstrate to the focus child exactly what to do. Take each part of the game in turn, either being a leader or taking a turn, so that the children get a full picture of what to do.
2. Starting the activity with a child who is likely to be successful.
3. Sometimes children may be happier taking only part of a turn, because they find it difficult to remember everything that they are supposed to do all at once. It is often a good idea to let them take over at the end of the turn, rather than the start and possibly lose attention as you support the end. As the children become more familiar with the activity they will be able to take on more. This way of breaking actions into smaller steps is called backward chaining.

4. Children with social and communication difficulties, particularly those with autistic spectrum disorder, often have problems weighing up alternatives and making a choice. Many of the games will encourage them to do this but many are likely to need a little extra help. One way of working towards an understanding of what choice is about is to offer a forced alternative, or an 'obvious' choice. An example might be, 'What shall we have as a prize: a smartie or this bottle top?' The idea is then to move towards genuine choices. Begin with an easy either/or before moving onto larger numbers of alternatives, such as turning over cards in Pelmanism.

No amount of distant advice can replace the personal knowledge and insight of a dedicated and sympathetic helper. The idea behind this compilation is that children who have missed out on the joy of play and social communication should work towards a greater understanding in as natural a way as possible.

Games

Based on Non-Verbal Skills

Index

Non-Verbal Skills

I can . . .

Share a focus of attention

- ❑ Snap
- ❑ Pelmanism
- ❑ Kim's game
- ❑ Farmer's in the den
- ❑ Uno

Demonstrate listening and looking skills

- ❑ Joker
- ❑ Bingo
- ❑ Cookie jar song
- ❑ Bear hunt
- ❑ Letters in your name

Attract someone's attention

- ❑ Name game
- ❑ Balloon game
- ❑ Matthew, Mark, Luke and John
- ❑ Stations
- ❑ Remembering things about others

Understand and use facial expression

- ❑ Noisy shaker
- ❑ Pass the facial expression
- ❑ Photograph games
- ❑ Expressions bingo

Understand and use gesture and body posture

- ❑ Charades
- ❑ Miming game (birthday present)
- ❑ Spot the conductor

Play a role/pretend

- ❑ Pass the stick
- ❑ Pictionary play dough
- ❑ Who am I?

Show awareness of others

- ❑ Changes
- ❑ Tig

Listen and do

- ❑ Run to the mat
- ❑ Simon says

Games

NON-VERBAL SKILLS
I CAN SHARE A FOCUS OF ATTENTION

Snap

Pelmanism

Kim's game

Farmer's in the den

Uno

SNAP

Key Skill
I can share a focus of attention

Cross Reference
I can demonstrate listening and looking skills

Other Skills
I can take turns
I can win or lose

Materials
A set of snap cards

How to Play
1. Simply explain the rules of the game as you set it up.

2. Demonstrate dealing the cards saying 'one for you, one for you, one for me', or using their names.

3. Take it in turns to place a card face up in a central pile.

4. Shout 'snap' when the top two cards are the same.

5. The winner gets all the cards in the middle and puts them underneath their own pile face down.

6. The game is over when there is only one person left with any cards.

Adaptations
To extend:
Each individual has their own pile of cards rather than one central pile. The 'snap' is when any two of the top cards are the same. This encourages children to look for information from different sources.

PELMANISM

Key Skill
I can share a focus of attention

Cross Reference
I can show awareness of others

Other Skills
I can take turns
I can win or lose

Materials
Sets of pairs pictures

How to Play
1. Simply explain the rules as you set up the game.

2. Place all the cards face down.

3. Take it in turns to turn two over.

4. Children keep a pair if they match.

5. You have another turn if you get one pair first time.

6. The winner is the player with the most pairs.

Adaptations
To simplify:
Use a grid or board to help the children organise the cards.

Note
Encourage the children to try and remember where they have seen cards to find pairs. It is helpful if cards are placed in the exact position.

KIM'S GAME

Key Skill
I can share a focus of attention

Cross Reference
I can show awareness of others

Other Skills
I can take turns
I can win or lose
I can choose
I can take the lead and follow others

Materials
A tray of everyday objects, e.g. keys, a cup, watch, toys etc. These could be on a theme, e.g. all beginning with the same letter, all to do with transport, music etc. Begin with six objects and then gradually increase it.

How to Play
1. The teacher shows the tray of objects to the group and asks them to try to remember them.

2. Each person works individually.

3. The teacher covers the tray with a cloth and removes it from view.

4. Pupils try to remember all the items.

Adaptations
To simplify:
Cover the items with a cloth and leave this in view so the pupils can see the outline of the items and have to guess what they are.

To extend:
Pupils are asked to work as a group and decide how they can help each other remember items.

Two groups can compete against each other.

Pupils discuss how they would like to play the game, e.g. individually, as a single group trying collectively to recall the items or in competitive groups.

Note
When first playing this game it is important to have items of interest to the pupil with social communication difficulties and it may be easier to let the group play individually at first.

FARMER'S IN THE DEN

Key Skill
I can share a focus of attention

Cross Reference
I can demonstrate listening and looking skills

Other Skills
I can take turns
I can choose
I can tolerate proximity

Materials
None needed

How to Play
1. Someone is the farmer.
2. The other children hold hands in a ring, with the farmer in the centre. They circle the farmer, chanting or singing:
   The farmer's in the den
   The farmer's in the den
   Ee Aye Adio
   The farmer's in the den.

   The farmer wants a wife etc. . . .
3. The farmer then has to choose someone from the circle to be the wife. This child joins the farmer in the middle of the circle and will make the next choice at the end of the next verse. This pattern continues until the song is over.
   The wife wants a child . . .
   The child wants a nurse . . .
   The nurse wants a dog . . .
4. During the last verse everybody crowds in to pat the dog, singing or chanting,
   We all pat the dog . . .

Notes
- Some children will want to give the dog a bone and pat that instead. This lacks authenticity in terms of helping children with social and communication difficulties understand social context.
- Children who are naturally boisterous may play more successfully if they stroke the dog, as opposed to patting!
- Some children, particularly those with social communication difficulties, may be frightened or distressed by the other children approaching and touching them at the end of this game. The patting or stroking could be substituted for:
  We all shout Hooray!
- Various methods can be used to choose the farmer. You could try election, who is wearing red, who is quietest, who can make the ugliest face, and so on.

UNO

Key Skill
I can share a focus of attention

Cross Reference
I can show awareness of others
I can give and receive information

Other Skills
I can take turns
I can win or lose

Materials
A commercial set of Uno cards (available in most toy shops and larger newsagents. Cost about £5–6).

How to Play
1. Explain the rules to the group.

2. Deal the cards equally among the group. Once the game has been played a few times a group member can do this.

3. Players place cards down in turn either matching the number or the colour of the previous card.

4. If certain cards are placed this means that the next player either misses a turn or the direction of the game is changed.

5. The game continues until one person has lost all their cards. They are the winner.

Adaptations
To simplify:
Remove the cards which indicate 'miss a go' and 'change direction' until the group are familiar with the game.

To extend:
Continue after the first person has won, until all the players have lost all their cards, giving each the opportunity to experience completion and discuss the positions in which they finished.

Games

NON-VERBAL SKILLS I CAN DEMONSTRATE LISTENING AND LOOKING SKILLS	
	Joker
	Bingo
	Cookie jar song
	Bear hunt
	Letters in your name

JOKER

Key Skill
I can demonstrate listening and looking skills

Cross Reference
I can share a focus of attention

Other Skills
I can win or lose
I can take turns

Materials
A set of playing cards or similar. You will need four of the same cards for each of the players (e.g. four queens, four kings, four aces).

How to Play
1. The cards are shuffled and dealt out evenly to each player.

2. The aim of the game is to have a matching set in your hand (e.g. four aces).

3. The first player discards one card and passes it upside down to the player on their left.

4. Play continues round the group until one player has four matching cards.

5. At this point the 'winner' says nothing but puts their finger on his or her nose.

6. If the other players notice they must do likewise.

7. Last one to notice is the 'joker'.

Adaptations
To extend:
When players become proficient at the game they can tease each other by scratching their face etc. as if they are about to touch their nose.

Notes
• The name 'joker' can be changed to whatever the players like.

• During the game use prompts to encourage looking and listening.

BINGO

Key Skill
I can demonstrate listening and looking skills

Cross Reference
I can share a focus of attention
I can understand and use facial expressions

Other Skills
I can win or lose

Materials
A set of Bingo cards, e.g. numbers, letters or pictures and felt tips to cross them off and corresponding single cards for the caller, e.g.

1	7	5
2	3	9

How to Play
1. The teacher acts as 'caller' and calls out the number, letter or picture which the player picks out. The caller holds the card close to their face to encourage eye contact.

2. The players cross out or cover the card called out.

3. The player to cross out or cover all their cards wins.

Adaptations
If using picture cards the student with social and communication difficulties may only be able to match a facial expression to a label of an emotion and further work could be too difficult. This must be respected.

COOKIE JAR SONG

Key Skill
I can demonstrate listening and looking skills

Cross Reference
I can share a focus of attention
I can attract someone's attention
I can use and understand gesture and body posture
I can alter my style

Other Skills
I can take turns

Materials
The chant:
Who stole the cookie from the cookie jar? Number one stole the cookie from the cookie jar.
Who me?
Yes, you.
Couldn't have been.
Then who?
Number two stole the cookie from the cookie jar . . . etc.

How to Play
1. Number the people in the group one, two, three . . .

2. Adult begins demonstrating the chant choosing a child who will find it easy to copy and join in.

3. Chant continues around the group, first in order and then in randomly chosen sequence.

Adaptations
Change the volume or the pitch to add interest.

To extend:
Make up different names for the people in the group in place of numbers.

Make up different rhymes based on the same structure, e.g. Who stole the frog from the garden pond? Be as humorous as you can. Give the children the chance to do likewise.

Note
Use prompts to encourage listening, responding and attention getting and role reversal.

BEAR HUNT

Key Skills
I can demonstrate listening and looking skills

Cross Reference
I can share focus of attention
I can use and understand gesture and body posture
I can alter my style

Other Skills
I can take the lead and follow others

Materials
The chant

How to Play
1. Let's go on a bear hunt . . . (clapping thighs and hands)
    We're going to find a big one
    Let's go . . . (continue clapping)
    Uh-oh!
    It's a . . . (various obstacles, e.g. river, bridge, mountain, swamp, grassy
    field, forest). We can't go over it, we can't go round it, we can't go under
    it, we'll have to go through it . . . (make up various noises and hand
    movements for each one, e.g. swimming, banging fists on chest, slow or
    fast thighs and hands clapping, swishing, 'it's dark in here', etc.)
2. The last place you get to is a cave.
3. You get to the cave and then build up the tension and suddenly roar . . .
    Then you go back through all the obstacles in reverse order as fast as
    you can.

Adaptations
To extend:
Alter the style to fit the 'obstacle' or bring in new 'obstacles' to add to the
range of styles.

The style can be altered by using a different animal (e.g. a squirrel or
kangaroo), different places to cross and using different ways (movements
and noises) to cross them.

LETTERS IN YOUR NAME

Key Skills
I can demonstrate listening and looking skills

Cross Reference
I can share a focus of attention

Other Skills
I can take turns
I can win or lose

Materials
None needed

How to Play
1. Someone is the caller.

2. The other children stand in a line facing them, about 3–5 metres away.

3. The caller says a letter of the alphabet.

4. If that letter is in their name then the pupil can take a step forward (or steps, if they have more than one of that letter).

5. Letters are called out randomly, mixing up vowels and consonants.

6. The first one to reach the caller becomes the caller in a new game.

Adaptations
To extend:
Use forenames, surnames, or both.

Allow jumps as well as steps.

Notes
*   Children unsure of spelling their name mentally, or whose processing may be too slow, could have a name card to help them check.

*   If some children appear to be rigging the game so that friends can win, try using a list of letters instead.

*   Use prompts to encourage looking and listening, and to deal with winning and losing.

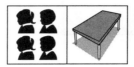

Games

NAME GAME

Key Skill
I can attract someone else's attention

Cross Reference
I can alter my style
I can demonstrate listening and looking skills

Other Skills
I can choose
I can take the lead and follow others

Materials
A bean bag or large soft sponge ball

How to Play
1. The children and any adults sit in a large circle.

2. The person with the ball or bean bag shouts out another person's name and either throws the bean bag or rolls the ball to that person.

3. The child receiving the bean bag or ball may need to be prompted to attend to the ball/bean bag coming towards them and to receive it.

4. The game should continue until each child has had their name called out on at least one occasion.

Adaptations
A fun version of this game is to use a plastic plate and play 'spin the plate'. This requires the child who is 'on' spinning a plate in the centre of the circle and shouting out another child's name. The other child has to try and reach the plate before it stops spinning and is flat on the floor.

Notes
• Either prior to or during the game you may need to discuss the volume of children's voices. They need to project their voices in this game.

• Use teacher prompts to encourage listening, looking, making choices, attracting attention.

BALLOON GAME

Key Skill
I can attract someone's attention

Cross Reference
I can demonstrate listening and looking skills

Other Skills
I can take turns
I can tolerate proximity

Materials
A balloon

How to Play
1. The group sit on chairs in a large circle.

2. The adult pats a balloon into the air and calls out the name of one of the children.

3. That child jumps up, pats the balloon up again and calls out another name.

4. The object of the game is to avoid the balloon hitting the floor.

Adaptations
A light beach ball could be used instead of a balloon.

Children could be seated on the floor.

Note
Use prompts to encourage listening, looking, attracting attention, taking turns.

MATTHEW, MARK, LUKE AND JOHN

Key Skills
I can attract someone's attention

Cross Reference
I can share a focus of attention
I can demonstrate listening and looking skills

Other Skills
I can take turns
I can win or lose
I can choose
I can anticipate

Materials
None

How to Play
1. Four children sit in a straight line, with the remainder of the children in another line.

   i.e. x   x x x x
       x
       x
       x

2. The children are given names and numbers in their lines, the vertical line being assigned Matthew, Mark, Luke and John and the horizontal line numbers one, two, three, four, etc.

3. Verbal messages in the form of a name and number are passed between each line, i.e. 'Matthew to two, two to John'. The rules are that messages cannot be passed directly back to the person or number who sent it. Should this happen, then the individual who has broken the rule must go to the end of the number line and everyone else moves along one space, remembering they have now acquired a new name or number.

4. The game ends after a specified time limit, determined at the onset.

Adaptations
To extend:
Children do not have to move if the rule is broken, they could receive penalty points instead.

Imposing a time limit to respond can be introduced.

Note
The adult may need to prompt children to respond quickly.

STATIONS

Key Skills
I can attract someone's attention

Cross Reference
I can demonstrate listening and looking skills

Other Skills
I can choose
I can win or lose

Materials
None needed

How to Play
1. The teacher demonstrates the game with two other children, explaining the rules.

2. The children sit in a circle with the teacher.

3. One person chooses a category, e.g. stations, fruit, vegetables.

4. Each person takes it in turn to choose an item from that category. This becomes their 'name' for the duration of the game.

5. One chair is taken away, leaving a person who is 'It' (or 'On').

6. This lead person shouts out the 'names' of two people. They have to swap chairs by running across the circle.

7. The person who is 'It' attempts to reach one of these chairs first. Whoever is left without a chair is 'It' and the game continues.

Adaptations
Variations in the categories chosen allows the game to be used to develop skills in categorisation.

Notes
- The teacher has a role in supporting children in remembering their own and others names, e.g. by suggesting a quick recap at any point.

- The teacher will need to maintain the pace of the game. It is the speed at which it is played which contributes to the fun.

- Children may need support in making quick choices.

REMEMBERING THINGS ABOUT OTHERS

Key Skill
I can attract someone's attention

Cross Reference
I can demonstrate listening and looking skills
I can give and receive information
I can alter my style

Other Skills
I can choose
I can remember important things about people

Materials
None needed

How to Play
1. The children and any adults sit in a large circle.

2. Each person in the circle takes it in turn to speak.

3. They start with a set phrase introduced by the group leader and complete it with their own sentence. Ideas for rounds include: 'My name is _____' 'My favourite food is _____' 'My favourite drink is _____' 'My favourite television programme is _____', etc.

4. When three or four of these rounds have taken place the next round should be 'I like _____ and his favourite food is _____.'

Adaptations
You can play this game using different set phrases. The chosen topic can support curriculum work. For example if children's emotions are being discussed in the classroom the rounds can include: what makes people happy, sad, angry and what people do that make others happy, sad or angry, etc.

Note
Some children may have difficulty coming up with a creative response to the phrase. It may be appropriate in these situations to allow them to copy another person's response and over time move them towards stating their own preference.

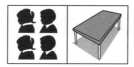  

Games

NON-VERBAL SKILLS	
I CAN UNDERSTAND AND USE FACIAL EXPRESSION	
	Noisy shaker
	Pass the facial expression
	Photograph games
	Expressions bingo

NOISY SHAKER

Key Skills
I can understand and use facial expression

Cross Reference
I can play a role/pretend

Other Skills
I can choose

Materials
Small, noise-making shaker (e.g. maraca or bell)

How to Play
1. One child leaves the room.

2. The other children stand or sit with their hands behind their backs.

3. One child is given the shaker.

4. When the child comes back into the room all of the children shake their hands as if they are playing the shaker. The child has to guess who has the shaker by reading people's facial expressions.

Adaptations
Other noisy items can be used instead of the shaker.

PASS THE FACIAL EXPRESSION

Key Skills
I can understand and use facial expression

Cross Reference
I can show awareness of others
I can give and receive information

Other Skills
I can take turns
I can tolerate proximity
I can anticipate

Materials
None needed

How to Play
1. The group sit in a circle (this may be round a table).

2. The leader expresses something with their face, e.g. demonstrates a really large smile.

3. The person on the leader's left is asked to look at this facial expression, copy it and then allow it to be copied by the person on their left.

4. The facial expression is passed all the way around the circle.

5. When it is the leader's turn again, after copying the last facial expression s/he can start a new one.

Adaptations
The facial expression might be deliberately chosen to match a particular emotion. The group could discuss which emotion they think it is.

The group might also choose to pull funny faces which are valid because they may require greater observational skills to copy.

Note
Try to play the game in silence during each 'round'.

PHOTOGRAPH GAMES

Key Skills
I can understand and use facial expression

Cross Reference
I can show awareness of others
I can give and receive information

Other Skills
I can take turns

Materials
A set of photographs cut out from magazines where the people in the photographs are expressing an obvious emotion and this is clear from their facial expression. There should be a balance of the emotions available, i.e. not all happy!, and a balance of ethnic origin and age. Once cut out, to make them last a little longer, it is best to mount them on card and laminate them, although this is not essential.

How to Play
Place the cards in a pile face down on the table. The group take it in turns to lift the card on top, show it to the others and identify the emotion.

Adaptations
Any variation on the following – use your imagination!

As above but instead of showing the card to the others the person who has picked the card up hides the card and copies the face so that the others can guess what the emotion on the card was.

Play Pelmanism with the cards. The pictures do not need to match, but the emotions do.

The person who picks up the card says 'This person is happy, I feel happy when _____'.

The person who picks the card up says 'This person is happy. I make my mum happy by _____'.

Pick the card up and draw on a piece of paper how that person is feeling. Show your paper to the rest of the group for them to guess the emotion.

Note
The games above become conceptually more difficult from beginning to end.

EXPRESSIONS BINGO

Key Skill
I can understand and use facial expression

Cross Reference
I can share a focus of attention
I can demonstrate listening and looking skills

Other Skills
I can win or lose

Materials
A set of facial expression cards, e.g. :) and corresponding individual cards

Happy	Frightened	Angry
Tired	Surprised	Sad

How to Play
1. The caller names an emotion e.g. happy, sad, angry.
2. The players match this to the facial expression on their card and cross it out or cover it up.
3. The player to cross out or cover up all of their cards wins.

Adaptations
To extend:
The caller 'pulls' the facial expression themselves and asks the players to match it to their facial expression bingo cards.

Players can take it in turn to be the caller.

The caller describes situations that will result in the emotion e.g., 'my dog died today so I feel '_____'.

Players take it in turns to be the caller, but may need prompt cards, e.g. 'someone said my hair looked stupid and I felt _____'.

Discussion about each emotion is important, e.g. some people may feel sad, others angry to the same situation.

Note
As the game progresses it becomes more complex and needs more analysis and sensitive handling due to the emotions involved. The players are encouraged to understand each other's point of view which may be different to their own.

Games

NON-VERBAL SKILLS

I CAN UNDERSTAND AND USE GESTURE AND BODY POSTURE

Charades

Miming game (birthday present)

Spot the conductor

CHARADES

Key Skills
I can understand and use gesture and body posture

Cross Reference
I can share a focus of attention
I can demonstrate listening and looking skills

Other Skills
I can win or lose
I can take turns
I can choose

Materials
None needed in the main game
Picture cards or pencil and paper for the adaptations

How to Play
1. The performer decides on a film, TV programme or a book.

2. They mime to the group to show which it is out of those three.

3. They hold up fingers to denote how many words there are in the title.

4. They show, by the number of fingers held up in turn, which word they are miming or portraying.

5. Children can guess the whole title at any time.

6. The winner takes over as performer.

Adaptations
To simplify:
A very basic game can be played using object or animal names or actions. If children cannot think of one for themselves, have a bag of picture cards so that they can do a lucky dip. Children with social communication difficulties may have a particular difficulty choosing something different from the one that went before.

Specific titles may help children to choose, e.g. Disney films.

More able children may like to write down a title each, pooling them all for a 'lucky dip' to choose one to enact.

MIMING GAME
(Birthday Present)

Key Skills
I can understand and use gesture and body posture

Cross Reference
I can share a focus of attention
I can give and receive information

Other Skills
I can ask for help and clarification

Materials
A cardboard box

How to Play
1. Set the scene, by explaining or demonstrating the game.

2. The lead person acts out the present that they are going to be putting in the box, pretends to wrap it and hands it over.

3. The receiver acts out how they feel about it as a present and what they are going to use it for.

4. Everyone takes a turn to be the giver and receiver.

Adaptations
The giver does not act out what is in the box, but just hands it over leaving the receiver to decide what the present is and how they feel about it.

Note
The teacher may need to provide the students with ideas for presents, either by brainstorming ideas before the game, giving picture clues or whispering possible items.

SPOT THE CONDUCTOR

Key Skills
I can understand and use gesture and body posture

Cross Reference
I can share a focus of attention

Other Skills
I can anticipate

Materials
None needed

How to Play
1. The teacher sends a small group of children out of the room.
2. She then chooses someone to be the 'conductor'.
3. All the rest of the children find a space in the hall but make sure they can see the conductor.
4. The conductor can do any body movement he or she likes and the rest of the group have to copy, e.g.

   arms up
   arms down
   jumping on the spot
   nodding head
   waving arms
   skipping
   tapping foot
   clapping hands

5. When the conductor has started the game, the teacher brings the children from outside back in.
6. They have to watch the group carefully and try to work out who the conductor is.
7. When they guess, another group goes out and the game continues.

Adaptations
This can be played with the children sitting in a circle and doing smaller movements with hands and using facial expressions.
It can also be played with a small group, one person being sent out at a time.

Note
Children may need to be given lots of ideas of movements they can do so they do not 'dry up' before being 'spotted'. The teacher may need to model this at first and possibly brainstorm and write down lots of ideas on a poster for the conductors to refer to.

Games

PASS THE STICK

Key Skill
I can play a role/pretend

Cross Reference
I can demonstrate listening and looking skills

Other Skills
I can take turns
I can win or lose

Materials
A stick or pencil

How to Play
1. The pupils sit in a circle.

2. The teacher starts the game by pretending the stick is something else.

3. The pupils have to guess what it is meant to be.

    Ideas for mimes are:

    - A broom
    - A spade
    - A paintbrush
    - A hairbrush
    - A mirror
    - A walking stick
    - A conductor's baton
    - A pen
    - A vacuum cleaner
    - A razor
    - A knife, fork or spoon
    - A telephone, etc.

4. The person who guesses correctly takes the next turn to mime.

Adaptations
To simplify:
If the pupils find it hard to mime something, some picture cards could be on hand to provide suggestions.

To extend:
Pupils can be split into teams and play competitively for points, the team that comes up with the most ideas wins the round.

Other objects can be used, e.g. a ball.

Eventually the stick can represent more abstract objects, e.g. a tennis racket, a gear stick.

This game can be extended into Charades.

PICTIONARY PLAY DOUGH

Key Skill
I can play a role/pretend

Cross Reference
I can give and receive information
I can understand and use gesture and body posture

Other Skills
I can win or lose

Materials
Play dough and as many chopping boards as you have teams
A list of words

How to Play
1. Explain the game.

2. Each team has up to six members and needs some play dough.

3. Each team sits in a small group, away from the others.

4. The teacher has a list of words.

5. Each team sends a representative to find out the word and goes back to their group to make it out of play dough. The representative can model the dough or act out the meaning of the word with it.

6. When the team guesses the word, another representative goes to the teacher for the next word.

7. The team that wins is the one that gets to the bottom of the word list first.

Adaptations
The teacher relates the word list to the curriculum or topic.

The teacher relates the word list to a specific class of word, e.g. nouns, proper nouns, verbs, adjectives, adverbs, prepositions.

Note
It is useful to have a 'helper' supporting the groups if they get stuck to reduce frustrations. The group needs to shout for help and 'the helper' then gives clues either to the 'modeller' or 'guessers'.

WHO AM I?

Key Skill
I can play a role/pretend

Cross Reference
I can give and receive information
I can understand and use gesture and body posture

Other Skills
I can remember important things about other people

Materials
Cards with clear descriptions of someone known to the children, such as a very famous footballer, the head teacher, etc. The name of the person should be written on the back of the card.

How to Play
1. The group leader explains the game and then reads out the description on one of the cards.

2. The children have to try and guess who is being described.

Adaptations
The teacher could act out the person's characteristics in a similar way to 'Charades'. The children could then also try doing this. Eventually they could come up with their own ideas of people.

Notes
- The cards and actions must be positive – they should not pick on anybody's weak points.

- The children may have trouble thinking of people to make statements about for themselves, whom the other children also know. If this is the case continue to suggest people to the group.

Games

NON-VERBAL SKILLS

I CAN SHOW AWARENESS OF OTHERS

Changes

Tig

CHANGES

Key Skill
I can show awareness of others

Cross Reference
I can demonstrate listening and looking skills

Other Skills
I can take turns
I can remember important things about other people

Materials
None needed for the main game
Props, such as dressing up clothes, hats and stickers, can be used to support the adaptation.

How to Play
1. Someone is the performer.

2. He or she leaves the room.

3. While out, the performer alters one aspect of appearance or clothing.

4. The performer comes back into the room.

5. The group has to look carefully to decide what has been changed.

6. The first person to spot the changes becomes the next performer.

Adaptations
To simplify:
Start with very obvious changes so that the children build up an understanding of the game.

To extend:
Increasing the subtlety will be fun.
Props, such as dressing up clothes, hats and hair bands, can be used to help with the change.
Making more than one change.

Notes
* Some children will need help in thinking what to change about themselves.

* If the group is struggling, there is an opportunity to direct attention by giving cues, e.g. using locational language, 'Simon has a ____ on his shirt', 'under his chin', and so on.

TIG

Key Skill
I can show awareness of others

Cross Reference
I can demonstrate listening and looking skills
I can attract someone's attention

Other Skills
I can win or lose
I can tolerate proximity

Materials
None needed

How to Play
1. Someone is 'on'.

2. The other children run away and try not to be tigged or touched.

3. The person who is 'on' tries to 'tig' them.

4. If a child is tigged, they become 'on' and the game continues.

5. The game is over after a pre-determined time limit.

Adaptations
To extend:
Try election to choose who is 'on'. Who is wearing a blue jumper, the smallest, who can make the funniest face, etc.

Play 'Scarecrow Tig' whereby the child who is tigged stands still with legs apart and arms out to the sides. They are then 'freed' by other children who have not been tigged crawling between their open legs. They can be encouraged to call the names of the other children to come and free them.

Chain Tig involves the children who have been tigged joining hands together and all being freed at the same time.

Notes
• If the space is large or a lot of people are playing you could have a team of 'catchers'.

• Some children will have difficulty keeping up with the pace. Use a time limit of a couple of minutes.

Games

NON-VERBAL SKILLS
I CAN LISTEN AND DO
Run to the mat
Simon says

RUN TO THE MAT

Key Skill
I can listen and do

Cross Reference
I can share a focus of attention

Other Skills
I can anticipate
I can tolerate proximity
I can win or lose
I can take the lead and follow others

Materials
A mat to mark a gathering space

How to Play
1. Someone needs to be in control, this is likely to be the group leader, but could be a member of the group.

2. A mat is laid out towards one end of the space.

3. The leader gives the group a key word or phrase, e.g. 'All aboard!'

4. When this phrase is called the group must run to the mat.

5. The leader gives the group instructions such as 'dance', 'sit down', or 'jump' using a casual voice. There may be need to give enough time so that children can take a cue from what their peers are doing.

6. All of a sudden the leader will call 'All aboard!' in an excited voice, whereupon the children all run to the mat.

7. The children then leave the mat and the game starts again.

Adaptations
The children could travel to the mat in different ways, e.g. jumping, hopping or crawling, although the tempo should be exciting.

The key phrase can be changed between rounds when the children are used to playing the game. Other phrases could be 'Scramble!', 'Let's go!' or 'Action!'

The last person to reach the mat is 'out' and the person left at the end is the winner.

Notes
- The change of tone and urgency in the leader's voice on calling the key phrase is important to give the children experience of how tone and intonation can influence response.

- This game is sometimes played by running to a wall, but this is unwise on the grounds of health and safety.

SIMON SAYS

Key Skill
I can listen and do

Cross Reference
I can demonstrate listening and looking skills

Other Skills
I can win or lose

Materials
None needed

How to Play
1. This is played as the traditional game. The teacher starts the game as the leader and explains the rules to the group.

2. The leader gives out the instructions preceded by the phrase 'Simon says'.

3. If the leader says 'Simon says' then everyone must do as they say. If not they must not follow the instruction.

4. Examples of instructions are:
   'Simon says put your hands on your head'
   'Simon says say hello'
   'Wave bye bye'

5. If a child doesn't follow the instruction correctly they are 'out'.

6. The winner is the person who is left 'in' at the end, they then become Simon.

Note
Children can take it in turns to be Simon, so all children have a turn, not just the winners. The teacher will need to be the judge of who is in or out and their word is final.

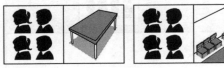

Games
Based on Verbal Skills

Verbal Skills

I can . . .

Say what I want and don't want

- ❏ Shopping game
- ❏ Pizza collage
- ❏ Mr Shark the shopkeeper

Start and finish talking to other people

- ❏ Asking for directions
- ❏ Twenty questions
- ❏ Speech bubbles with cartoons
- ❏ Hello and goodbye

Maintain a topic

- ❏ Just a minute
- ❏ Sentence making
- ❏ ABC games
- ❏ Guess the category
- ❏ Word association
- ❏ Robot madness

Give and receive information

- ❏ Telephone game
- ❏ What's the time Mr Wolf?
- ❏ Barrier games (e.g. Battleships)
- ❏ Happy families
- ❏ The man from Mars
- ❏ Blindfold directions
- ❏ Mr Frog

Say what I like and don't like

- ❏ Tasting game
- ❏ Feeling game
- ❏ Smelling game
- ❏ Music game
- ❏ Picture critique
- ❏ I like you because . . .
- ❏ Stargazing
- ❏ My name, her name
- ❏ I like it too

Alter my style

- ❏ Chinese whispers
- ❏ Animal magic
- ❏ Adverb game

Apologise

- ❏ Sorry
- ❏ Ladders

Games

SHOPPING GAME

Key Skill
I can say what I want and don't want

Cross Reference
I can play a role/pretend

Other Skills
I can choose
I can take turns

Materials
Use the published game 'Let's go shopping' or make up your own using boxes to represent various shops including: greengrocer, supermarket, shoe shop, chemist, etc. Collect pictures from magazines to go with each shop.

How to Play
If using the published game follow directions and play as normal. If using the home-made game:

1. Ask the children to sort out the pictures to the appropriate shop.

2. The children then role play their shopping trip, one at a time visiting each shop and choosing an item. At each shop the teacher asks 'What would you like?' or 'Can I help you?'

Adaptations
To simplify:
Specify that one item must be chosen from each shop.

To extend:
The children themselves can role play being shopkeepers.

The children can make a list of what they would like to buy before they get to the shops. This means they may have to decide on the 'next best thing' if what they want is unavailable.

Note
The aim of the game is for the children to be able to say what they want and don't want, not to be able to remember long lists of shopping.

PIZZA COLLAGE

Key Skills
I can say what I want and don't want

Cross Reference
I can show awareness of others

Other Skills
I can win or lose
I can choose

Materials
Collage materials representing a pizza base and basic pizza ingredients.
These do not have to be exact, but could be symbolic, e.g. yellow squares
as pineapple, yellow circles as sweetcorn, a red crayon to draw the sauce,
etc.

How to Play
1. Explain the aim of the game is to describe to the pizza chef exactly what
   you want on your pizza.

2. The children get into pairs, a chef and a customer.

3. Each customer chooses from the array of toppings, what they want or
   don't want and tells the pizza chef who makes it for them.

4. The chef and the customer work together as a team to get as many
   toppings on the pizza as possible in 30 seconds. One point for each
   topping.

5. The winning team is the one with the most points.

Adaptations
A group could make one pizza between them, enabling them to negotiate
the choice of toppings.

Note
The number of potential toppings can be amended at the teacher's
discretion.

MR SHARK THE SHOPKEEPER

Key Skills
I can say what I want and don't want

Cross Reference
I can play a role/pretend
I can show awareness of others

Other Skills
I can choose
I can win or lose
I can anticipate

Materials
A collection of coins. Play money will do for some, but others may need to use real coins.
A collection of articles for sale
Price tags

How to Play
1. The adult will usually be Mr Shark.
2. Mr Shark sits behind a table, on which his wares are displayed, clearly price tagged.
3. The pupil has a sum of money and has to choose what to buy.
4. Mr Shark tries to influence the choice, in his oily and ingratiating manner.
5. Once the choice is made, Mr Shark tries to deceive the pupil about the cost, perhaps by covering the price label with his hand, or announcing it wrongly.
6. If discovered, Mr Shark makes an ingratiating apology, blaming his eyesight or his poor memory.
7. A score can be kept as to who has 'won' the most encounters.

Adaptations
To extend:
Mr Shark can cheat in a variety of ways. He can simply announce the wrong price. He can give the wrong change, counting it out wrongly into the pupil's hand. If more than one article is purchased, he can total the cost wrongly.

Mr Shark can simply ask for the money, giving no goods in return, e.g. 'That's a nice, shiny 10p'. 'Better let me look after it for you'. 'I'll put it in the box for the poor children', and so on.

Mr Shark can try to distract the pupil with irrelevancies, such as 'How is your dear mother?'

Children enjoy pretending to come into the room, making a ding-dong as the door opens. Mr Shark may welcome them with his oily smile and his outstretched hand.

Notes
- Some children benefit from the use of a calculator or ruler to help them to work out their change. Others may need pencil and paper.
- Mr Shark comes out of role to help the children. This is why strong visual cues and a different voice are important, so that the children know which role you are in.

Games

VERBAL SKILLS

I CAN START AND FINISH TALKING TO OTHER PEOPLE

Asking for directions

Twenty questions

Speech bubbles with cartoons

Hello and goodbye

ASKING FOR DIRECTIONS

Key Skills
I can start and finish talking to other people

Cross Reference
I can give and receive information
I can alter my style
I can play a role/pretend

Other Skills
I can ask for help and clarification
I can remember important things about other people

Materials
A set of cards depicting people/places in the school

How to Play
1. Introduce the game by brainstorming, describing or acting out with toys what you need to do if you can't find somewhere.
2. Demonstrate with two adults how to ask for directions to places within the school.
3. Assign roles   A   You are the teacher
                    B   You are a new child
4. The person in role A has to pick a card with the name of a person or place on it. They need to get to this place. Use pictures if the children cannot yet read.
5. A and B act out the roles of asking and giving directions.

Adaptations
Introduce different ways of beginning a conversation, e.g.

'Excuse me . . . How do I get to . . .'
'Mrs . . . Can you tell me where to find . . .'
'Can you help me? . . . I don't know where the . . . is'
Tap on the arm. 'I can't find . . .'

and different ways of ending it, e.g.

'Thank you'
'Oh that's great'
'I think I can find it now'
'That's a big help'
'Thanks, bye'

Assign different roles, e.g. friends, head teacher, a visitor asking a child, etc.

Act out standing too close or too far apart, or shouting or speaking too quietly, or not looking, etc. Ask the children to spot your mistakes and then each other's in the role play.

Introduce the idea of asking for a repetition of the direction, e.g. 'Sorry can you say that again?' and re-capping the directions together using gesture.

Introduce the idea of person B not knowing the answer and suggesting who they could speak to instead.

Note
Brainstorm safety aspects and who the children can approach safely.

TWENTY QUESTIONS

Key Skills
I can start and finish talking to other people

Cross Reference
I can give and receive information
I can demonstrate listening and looking skills

Other Skills
I can take turns
I can remember important things about other people
I can win or lose

Materials
A bag of objects or pictures

How to Play
1. Hide an object which will remain a secret until guessed.
2. Two adults model how to ask Yes/No questions to find out the identity of the object.
3. Children are reminded that they cannot ask directly what the object is and can only ask questions which can be answered by Yes/No.
4. Each child takes a turn at asking a question to which the adult responds Yes/No.
5. The game continues until the object is discovered, by someone saying 'I want to guess'.

Adaptations
To simplify:
The number of questions is restricted and counted down using an abacus or tally chart.

People known to the group, or famous people, or places can be substituted for objects.

The children can take turns in order by the place they are sitting or by putting up hands to ask a question.

To extend:
If the person guesses the object wrongly they are out.

Notes
- You can use symbol cards to prompt specific questions, e.g.
  Where is it kept?
  Who uses it?
  Can you (action) with it?
  Is it . . . (attribute)?
- You will need to teach the association between the question and the symbol, e.g.
  an action symbol for 'Can you . . . with it?'
  a 'look' symbol for questions about attributes
  a 'person' symbol for who uses it
  a 'where' symbol for where it is kept.

SPEECH BUBBLES WITH CARTOONS

Key Skills
I can start and finish talking to other people

Cross Reference
I can maintain a topic
I can give and receive information

Other Skills
I can take turns

Materials
Cartoons from everyday children's comics with the dialogue either hidden or erased. Empty speech bubbles can be drawn in advance. A set of written ways of starting or finishing talking to someone else which can be serious or funny such as:

Hello
Hi!
What are you doing here?
I'll see you later
Goodbye
Go away!

Focus on the start and finish of conversations or meetings of characters.

How to Play
1. Place the cartoons and the written 'remarks' down on the table.

2. The children match an opening or closing remark to each cartoon situation and then share it with the rest of the group. These can be very funny when the dialogue does not match the situation. While playing the teacher can encourage the children to notice which words are more or less appropriate to the situation and which ones they might use in real life.

Adaptations
To extend:
Ask the children to think of the opening and closing remarks rather than having them pre-prepared.

Note
Young children typically do not use formal ways to start and finish talking to others; notice the words the children use naturally and include these in the speech bubbles. You can include improbable captions too!

HELLO AND GOODBYE

Key Skills
I can start and finish talking to other people

Cross Reference
I can alter my style
I can play a role/pretend

Other Skills
I can take turns
I can ask for help and clarification

Materials
A set of cards with different scenarios printed on them (see Appendix A, p. 105)
A spinner

How to Play
1. Explain how to play the game.

2. Spread the cards out in a circle with the spinner in the middle.

3. The children take it in turns. The first child spins the spinner and reads out the scenario to which the spinner points when it stops. They may need help to read it. That child then picks a partner so in a pair they act out how to say hello and goodbye appropriately given the context.

4. There needs to be some discussion after each enactment about whether it was appropriate.

5. The spinner passes to the next person in the circle.

Note
Precede the game by talking about why we say hello and goodbye, and under what circumstances.

Games

VERBAL SKILLS		
I CAN MAINTAIN A TOPIC		
		Just a minute
		Sentence making
		ABC games
		Guess the category
		Word association
		Robot madness

JUST A MINUTE

Key Skill
I can maintain a topic

Cross Reference
I can start and finish talking to other people
I can demonstrate listening and looking skills

Other Skills
I can win or lose

Materials
None needed

How to Play
1. Everyone sits in a circle. The teacher explains the game, the aim of which is to stay on topic.

2. Choose someone to be 'on'.

3. This person chooses or is given something to talk about.

4. Everyone listens.

5. When the speaker makes a significant pause, the leader stops the game, indicating that the next person in the group should carry on with the same topic.

6. This is repeated throughout the game until a minute is up.

7. The person talking at the end of the minute is the winner.

8. The next game starts with the person on the winner's right.

Adaptations
Subjects can be drawn out of a bag, perhaps using pictures to help young children.

The time given can be altered, according to the concentration and processing skills of the players.

It may be appropriate to use a stopwatch to time the game, so that people thinking of what to say do not use the minute.

Note
Prompting can take the form of asking or reminding the players what had just been said or giving the individual a starting thought to link the subject to their own experience.

SENTENCE MAKING

Key Skill
I can maintain a topic

Cross Reference
I can share a focus of attention
I can demonstrate listening and looking skills

Other Skills
I can take turns
I can anticipate
I can choose

Materials
Pictures or objects as props

How to Play
1. The teacher demonstrates how to play the game with one student.

2. The first person starts the sentence with a single word.

3. Each person takes a turn at adding a word to form a sentence.

4. When the sentence is complete the last person says 'full stop'.

5. The idea is to make the longest or most amusing sentence, working together as a team.

Adaptations
To extend:
The teacher or lead student makes up the first phrase of the sentence which is then added to in the above way.

The students add sentences to form a narrative, rather than individual words.

Note
The teacher's role is to encourage the students to make grammatically correct logical sentences, e.g. by prompting the students to think about the meaning of what has gone before or offering them a choice of words. The picture/object props can be used to provide ideas to the students.

ABC GAMES

Key Skill
I can maintain a topic

Cross Reference
I can demonstrate listening and looking skills

Other Skills
I can take turns

Materials
None

How to Play
1. Simply explain the rules. Add items to a list.

2. The aim is to add in turn. These must follow alphabetical order and be appropriate to the topic, e.g. 'I went on holiday and I took . . . air tickets, beach towel, car keys,' etc.

Adaptations
Suggested topics could include:
I went to the café and I ate . . .
I went around the world and I visited . . .
I went to the moon and I took . . .

To simplify:
If following alphabetical order is too difficult allow the children to make any suggestions on the topic.

To extend:
Children can be encouraged to pick the topic.

Note
The teacher may need to intervene to recap what has gone before and to control the pace of the game.

GUESS THE CATEGORY

Key Skill
I can maintain a topic

Cross Reference
I can give and receive information

Other Skills
I can take turns
I can choose

Materials
Picture cards of items that belong together in categories such as vegetables, vehicles, tools, animals, etc. (at least five of each). For more difficult games categories such as items beginning with letter 'p', things that keep you warm, things that you find in the sea, etc.

How to Play
1. Each player takes it in turn to select a few pictures that go together in a category.

2. The others have to guess what it is about the pictures that make them a group, e.g. they are all vegetables, they are all things you wear, etc.

Note
The teacher will need to be the judge for this game as there may be some disputes as to whether items truly go together. However, if the player has a good reason this is usually enough.

WORD ASSOCIATION

Key Skill
I can maintain a topic

Cross Reference
I can demonstrate listening and looking skills
I can share a focus of attention

Other Skills
I can choose
I can take turns
I can win or lose

Materials
None needed

How to Play
1. Demonstrate how words are linked together in meaning with a number of examples.

2. One child leads by saying a word. The next person has to say a word related in meaning to the one that went before. The game continues round in a circle.

3. The round ends after a pre-determined time limit stated at the outset.

4. Individuals can challenge the association between words when the person who said that word must justify its choice. The child is out if they cannot justify their choice of word.

Adaptations
You could say a whole sentence each time rather than just one word.

The topic could be determined from the start and all words and sentences have to be related to that topic.

A ball or bean bag could be passed between the children. If they wish to specify a new category they must shout 'change' and the name of the new category when they have the ball.

Note
The children can be encouraged to get faster in their thinking time.

ROBOT MADNESS

Key Skills
I can maintain a topic

Cross Reference
I can give and receive information
I can play a role/pretend

Other Skills
I can take turns

Materials
A hat/helmet for the child playing the robot to wear. This is not essential.
Some pre-written tasks for the robot to perform, e.g.
    Fetching a book
    Switching on a light
    Taking a message to someone

How to Play
1. The leader selects a child to pretend to be the robot.

2. The leader explains to the children that the robot is not working properly.

3. They need to give it clear directions of what they want it to do.

4. The children take it in turns to tell the robot where they want it to go.

5. The robot gets all the instructions wrong.

Games

TELEPHONE GAME

Key Skill
I can give and receive information

Cross Reference
I can demonstrate listening and looking skills
I can alter my style
I can show awareness of others

Other Skills
I can remember important things about other people
I can take turns

Materials
An old telephone – a real one preferably.

How to Play
1. The adult has a pretend conversation with someone well known to the children, e.g. head teacher, a peer, famous person or a person with a particular occupation gradually giving hints as to who they are speaking to.

2. The children have to guess who is on the telephone and then take turns themselves pretending to talk to someone.

Adaptations
'Guess the situation'. The adult is called by someone, e.g. the police and reacts to the call. The children have to guess what is wrong. Each child has a turn at being called. If you have access to walkie talkies you could take turns being the police and the person taking the call.

Note
Always start by pretending to talk to someone important to the pupils. It may be too difficult for the pupils to pretend and use the appropriate level of inflection and language so the teacher will need to do all the talking at first.

WHAT'S THE TIME MR WOLF?

Key Skill
I can give and receive information

Cross Reference
I can show awareness of others
I can alter my style

Other Skills
I can anticipate
I can take turns
I can win or lose

Materials
None needed

How to Play
1. Choose someone to be 'on'.

2. This person stands facing a wall.

3. The other players line up some distance behind.

4. They call 'What's the time, Mr Wolf?' and take a step forward.

5. The wolf turns around and replies, e.g. 'One o'clock'.

6. This sequence is repeated throughout the game, with the players coming closer and closer to the wolf. Anyone caught moving by the wolf is sent back.

7. Eventually the wolf will shout 'Dinner Time!' in response to the question.

8. This is the signal for everyone to run. The wolf will try to catch someone for dinner.

9. The person that is caught will be the next wolf.

Adaptations
Another version of this game is called Ice Cream Van. Players are organised in the same way, but instead of calling out 'What's the time, Mr Wolf' and taking a step forward, the group approaches stealthily. The person who is on turns and, if they see anyone moving, orders them back to the starting point. The winner is the first to touch the ice cream van.

Various methods can be used to choose the first wolf. You could try election, who is wearing red, who is quietest, who can make the ugliest face, and so on.

Teasing can also be built into this game, by the wolf hesitating with an answer.

Notes
• Be aware that children may not run so fast if they want to be 'on'! It may be possible to substitute a forfeit for being caught so that everyone has a turn at being the wolf.

• Encourage the wolf to modulate tones, becoming very fierce about 'Dinner Time'.

• Children might like to hold hands as they approach.

• Some children may need a visual signal from you so they know when to call.

BARRIER GAMES (e.g. Battleships)

Key Skill
I can give and receive information

Cross Reference
I can demonstrate listening and looking skills
I can attract someone's attention

Other Skills
I can ask for help and clarification
I can take turns

Materials
Two sets of matching pictures, crayons, pencils, etc. or construction materials

How to Play
1. Explain the game. The purpose is to make matching pictures or construction at the end of the game.

2. Give each child the same set of materials, e.g. identical pictures and crayons, identical bricks, or construction materials. Put the barrier between them.

3. One child is the leader and this person gives the command, e.g. 'colour the clown's hat blue'. Both children do the action at the same time.

4. The children are encouraged to say when they have finished, or that they are not ready to continue yet, by the adult modelling these statements.

5. The children are encouraged to ask 'Are you finished yet?' or 'What next?', as appropriate, by the teacher modelling these at the appropriate time.

6. When the design has been completed the barrier is removed and the children compare their work.

Adaptations
To encourage statements rather than commands, one child is given a completed drawing or construction to describe.

To encourage questions the 'receiver' has to ask for information, e.g. 'Is the hat blue?', or 'What colour should I do the hat?'

The children are encouraged to expand their spoken language by giving two ideas linked by 'and'.

Published elimination games like Guess Who and Battleships.

Non-published games using logic blocks and logic people.

Note
To build in requests for clarification, the children are taught how to ask for a repetition or for a statement to be explained.

Phrases like 'Can you say that again', or 'I didn't hear' or 'I don't understand' are modelled by the teacher, and are then prompted, e.g. 'Do you understand what you have to do? No, well say "I don't understand" at the appropriate times.'

HAPPY FAMILIES

Key Skill
I can give and receive information

Cross Reference
I can demonstrate listening and looking skills
I can attract someone's attention

Other Skills
I can take turns
I can anticipate
I can win or lose

Materials
A set of Happy Families picture cards, e.g. animals, occupations, nationalities

How to Play
1. Simply explain the rules of the game – the object is to collect family sets; Mr, Mrs, Master and Miss. The player who collects the most sets is the winner.

2. Deal out the cards. Decide who is going to begin.

3. This person asks a player for a specific picture card.

4. Another turn is taken if they have the requested card.

5. Continue until the requested card is not available. The turn then passes to the next person.

Notes
• Show the children the 'families' before playing to familiarise them with the different characters.

• Encourage eye contact from each child when asking or responding to the questions.

THE MAN FROM MARS

Key Skill
I can give and receive information

Cross Reference
I can share a focus of attention
I can play a role/pretend

Other Skills
I can take turns
I can take the lead and follow others

Materials
Five common familiar objects, e.g. stamp, toothbrush, tissue, etc.

How to Play
1. The adult pretends to be an alien from another planet 'A man from Mars', who has just arrived on Earth and has never seen some of the Earth objects before. The alien does not know what to do with them. Enlist the children's aid in describing and explaining quite specifically what the objects are for and how to use them.

2. Ask about each object, one at a time.

3. Give each child the opportunity to describe and explain.

4. The adult must deliberately act 'stupid', or follow the children's directions literally in order to enable them to be more detailed in their explanation.

Adaptations
The children decide which planet the alien is from and make a relevant mask for the adult to wear.

To extend:
The alien could be trying to learn how to do something that involves a sequence of events, e.g. peeling an orange, getting a drink of water, blowing your nose.

The children can have a turn at being the alien.

Note
Be prepared to recap each stage of an explanation several times.

BLINDFOLD DIRECTIONS

Key Skill
I can give and receive information

Cross Reference
I can alter my style
I can demonstrate listening and looking skills
I can show awareness of others

Other Skills
I can choose
I can take turns
I can win or lose

Materials
A blindfold
Start and finish cards

How to Play
1. Push all the furniture in the classroom to the side apart from one or two large pieces of equipment.

2. Mark a point in the classroom with the start card and another point with the finish card.

3. One child is blindfolded and stands at the start.

4. Another child stands at the finish point and gives the blindfolded child directions to get to the finish avoiding the equipment.

Adaptations
To extend:
Time the pairs of children. The winning pair is the one that takes the least time.

Notes
- Some children do not like to be blindfolded. Do not insist.

- If the child giving directions is unable to reverse his/her rights and lefts they could stand at the start so that they are facing the same way as the blindfolded child.

- Make the obstacle course easy to start with and increase the difficulty.

- Avoid things which could hurt the blindfolded child.

- Discuss appropriate voice volume with the child giving directions.

- Discuss with the group prior to starting the sort of commands that could be used.

MR FROG

Key Skill
I can give and receive information

Cross Reference
I can demonstrate listening and looking skills
I can play a role/pretend

Other Skills
I can take turns
I can remember important things about other people
I can take the lead and follow others

Materials
None

How to Play
1. One child is Mr Frog and sits on a 'lily pad' at one end of the room.

2. The other children and an adult sit on a row of chairs at the other end.

3. Children chant 'Mr Frog, Mr Frog can I have some of your . . .?' Mr Frog replies 'Only if you have . . .', e.g. blue trousers, wearing a watch, a name beginning with D.

4. Each child to whom that applies takes a step towards the lily pad. The chant is repeated and the frog chooses another description.

5. The first child to reach the 'lily pad' takes over as Mr Frog.

Adaptations
To extend:
The children can volunteer to be Mr Frog.

Note
Children may need prompting to ask questions of Mr Frog.

Games

VERBAL SKILLS

I CAN SAY WHAT I LIKE AND DON'T LIKE

Tasting game

Feeling game

Smelling game

Music game

Picture critique

I like you because . . .

Stargazing

My name, her name

I like it too

TASTING GAME

Key Skill
I can say what I like and don't like

Cross Reference
I can show awareness of others

Other Skills
I can remember important things about other people

Materials
A variety of foods for the children to taste,* from bland to spicy flavours, e.g.

- fruit pieces of: orange, banana, apple, kiwi, grapefruit, lemon, etc.

- powdered spices: cinnamon, curry powder, garam masala, ginger, also plain powdered items such as flour, sugar, salt.

- samples of breakfast cereals.

- vegetables, pieces of: carrot, onion, garlic, parsnip, etc.

- Paper and pencil.

How to Play
There are two ways to play.

1. The children taste all the food items and decide what they like and don't like. The teacher can point out that all the children's likes and dislikes are different. This can be recorded on a chart.

2. The children can taste the food blindfolded and say whether they recognise it and whether they like it or not.

* Check the children have no food allergies first.

Adaptations
Ask the children (quietly) what their favourite dinner would be and make a list of these. At the end of the session read out the list one by one and see if the group can guess who the favourite dinner 'belongs' to.

Notes
- Make sure that individual children's opinions are valued if they are different to the majority view.

- Model appropriate ways of saying 'I don't like it'. There may be an opportunity to discuss how to refuse politely.

FEELING GAME

Key Skill
I can say what I like and don't like

Cross Reference
I can show awareness of others
I can give and receive information
I can share a focus of attention

Other Skills
I can take turns

Materials
* A traditional 'feelie bag' containing items of different shapes and textures, e.g.

>marble
>coin
>toothbrush
>orange
>spoon
>some wire wool
>sponge

or

a blindfold and items of different textures as above and including soap, play dough and play slime

How to Play
1. Ask the children, one by one to put their hand on an item and feel it and describe their response to it.

2. The game can become a guessing game to the description of the item but that it is not the main aim of the game.

3. Make a chart of the children's likes and dislikes.

Adaptations
(see smelling, tasting and music games)

Note
Make sure individual children's opinions are valued if they are different to the majority view.

* Check the children have no allergies.

SMELLING GAME

Key Skill
I can say what I like and don't like

Cross Reference
I can show awareness of others
I can share a focus of attention

Other Skills
I can remember important things about other people

Materials
A range of items that have a variety of smells, e.g.

> perfumes
> onion
> tinned fish
> flowers
> garlic
> coffee

A blindfold (do not insist the child wears a blindfold if they refuse)

How to Play
1. Ask the children to smell each item in turn, see and say how they feel about it.

2. You may like to make a chart to show the children's preferences.

3. The children can guess the object, but this is not the main aim of the game.

Adaptations
Make a collection of different perfumes/after shave lotion (empty bottles will do). You can buy sets from the RNIB.

See what the children like and dislike.

Ask the children for their favourite smell and their worst smell. See if they can remember each other's favourite/worst smells.

Note
Make sure that individual children's opinions are valued if they are different to the majority view.

MUSIC GAME

Key Skill
I can say what I like and don't like

Cross Reference
I can show awareness of others

Other Skills
I can remember important things about other people

Materials
Tape/CD player
Tapes or CDs of a variety of styles of music
Pencils and paper

How to Play
1. Ask the children to listen to five pieces of music, some familiar, some unfamiliar and after each one to say whether they liked it or not. Ask for opinions on the style of music, and volume, etc.

2. This can be recorded on a chart.

3. Ask the children to listen to an unfamiliar piece of music again and see if any of them change their minds.

Adaptations
Ask the children to bring in their favourite music to play to the others. Note the different reactions from the children. The following session see if they can remember each other's preferences.

Notes
- Make sure individual opinions are respected.

- Explain that preferences for music can change with opportunity to experience different styles.

PICTURE CRITIQUE

Key Skill
I can say what I like and don't like

Cross Reference
I can show awareness of others

Other Skills
I can win or lose

Materials
A set of pictures, one drawn by each member of the group

How to Play
1. Explain to the children that they will be looking at each other's work, and describing what they like about it.

2. You will need to discuss with the children how they will react if they receive a compliment.

   You will need to discuss and perhaps role play how to give and receive compliments.

3. Let the children see all the pictures as a gallery and give them time to develop their opinions.

4. Ask each child individually to give their opinions on what they have seen, asking what they like and why.

Adaptations
A grading system could be used to decide which is the best picture overall. The pictures used could be commercially available posters, or pictures from magazines. This would avoid any perceived threat of receiving personal criticism, while allowing the child to express what they do not like.

Note
Teachers need to be prepared to guide children's thinking in terms of how the pictures make them feel, identifying more specifically what it is they do or do not like.

I LIKE YOU BECAUSE . . .

Key Skill
I can say what I like and don't like

Cross Reference
I can demonstrate listening and looking skills
I can alter my style

Other Skills
I can choose
I can remember important things about other people

Materials
None needed

How to Play
1. The children and any adults sit in a large circle.

2. Each person in the circle takes it in turn to speak. They start with a set phrase introduced by the group leader and complete it with their own sentence. Ideas for rounds include: 'I like to read books about _____', 'When I get home I like to _____', 'My favourite place to go out is _____'.

3. When three or four of these rounds have taken place the next round should be 'I like _____ because _____'.

Notes
- Some children may have difficulty coming up with a creative response to the phrase. It may be appropriate in these situations to allow them to copy another person's response and over time move them towards stating their own preference.

- Try to engineer it so that every child is liked by someone – adults can select the less popular children.

STARGAZING

Key Skill
I can say what I like and don't like

Cross Reference
I can share a focus of attention

Other Skills
I can choose

Materials
Pictures of stars (film, pop, football magazines)

How to Play
1. Explain that the children will be looking at pictures of these stars and describing what they do or do not like about them and why.

2. You will need to discuss with the children how they will react if someone criticises a star they like. It may be necessary to role play this.

3. Let the children see all the posters or pictures and give them some time to develop their opinions.

4. Ask each child individually to say what they think about each one and why.

Adaptations
To reduce the amount of time involved, each child could compliment one person and criticise another.

Note
Teachers must be prepared to guide children's thinking in terms of who they like or don't like and why.

MY NAME, HER NAME

Key Skill
I can say what I like and don't like

Cross Reference
I can demonstrate listening and looking skills
I can show awareness of others

Other Skills
I can take turns

Materials
A large sheet of flip chart paper and a selection of felt pens

How to Play
1. Everyone sits in a large circle.

2. Each person in the circle takes it in turn to write their name on the paper. They should then say whether or not they like their name and why.

3. After this round, go around the circle where the children say which other names they like and why.

Note
Try to engineer it so that every child's name is liked by someone, even if they don't like their own name – adults can select the less popular children's names.

I LIKE IT TOO

Key Skill
I can say what I like and don't like

Cross Reference
I can share a focus of attention
I can demonstrate listening and looking skills

Other Skills
I can take turns
I can remember important things about other people

Materials
A set of cards with objects/events on, e.g. a roller coaster, crocodiles, going to the farm. Several different sets of coloured counters, one set for each child in the game.

How to Play
1. Explain that the game is about finding out reasons why we like things.

2. The first child turns over a card from the pile and reads it aloud. Help may be needed with reading.

    They must give a reason why they like that object or event and put a counter down in front of them. A counter can only be placed down if they have a reason.

3. Each child takes a turn to think of a reason why they also like that object/event and places a counter down until the round is completed.

4. The next child turns over the next card and the game continues.

5. If a child cannot think of a new reason he/she says 'pass'.

6. The winner is the child who gets rid of all his/her counters first.

Adaptations
The game can be altered to enable children to say what they don't like about an event/object.

Note
The teacher may need to take a role in helping the children to value each other's opinions.

Games

VERBAL SKILLS

I CAN ALTER MY STYLE

Chinese whispers

Animal magic

Adverb game

CHINESE WHISPERS

Key Skill
I can alter my style

Cross Reference
I can understand and use gesture and body posture

Other Skills
I can ask for help and clarification
I can take turns
I can take the lead and follow others

Materials
Chairs

How to Play
The teacher explains simply how to play and demonstrates.

1. The teacher thinks of a short sentence and whispers it to the first child.

2. This child copies this model to the second child.

3. The message goes round in a circle.

4. The last person says it out loud.

5. The group discuss where it went wrong.

Adaptations
To simplify:
Each child has a turn thinking of a sentence.

Draw a set of pictures and collect a set of corresponding objects.

The first person chooses a card and describes the picture, e.g. 'The cat is on the table.'

The last person performs the task, i.e. puts the cat on the table, and compares this with the picture.

Everybody discusses whether the picture and constructions look the same.

Note
Children may need prompting to remember to whisper, to sit close enough, to ask for repetition.

ANIMAL MAGIC

Key Skill
I can alter my style

Cross Reference
I can understand and use gesture and body posture
I can understand and use facial expression
I can play a role/pretend

Other Skills
I can take turns

Materials
A set of cards with animal names (and/or pictures)

How to Play
1. One at a time let the children choose a card.

2. The child must act out the behaviour of that particular animal when eating and moving.

3. The other children must guess which animal it is.

4. Move around the group until each child has had a turn at being an animal.

Adaptations
Brainstorm a set of animals at the beginning and let the children make their own cards.

Notes
- Help the children to envisage the animal in its environment.
- Ensure the child miming does not say the animal name.

ADVERB GAME

Key Skill
I can alter my style

Cross Reference
I can play a role/pretend
I can demonstrate listening and looking skills

Other Skills
I can take turns

Materials
Cue cards with a number of different adverbs written on them

How to Play
1. The teacher demonstrates a chosen action in a variety of different ways, the manner changing with each adverb, e.g. roughly, quietly, grumpily.

2. The group chooses a particular action they will mime.

3. The children take it in turns to choose a cue card and mime the action as per the adverb on the card.

4. The group guesses the adverb.

5. Go round the group until everyone has had a turn.

Adaptations
A set of cards with different activities to be mimed could be used, but the children will need to say what they are miming as the object of the game is only to guess how.

To extend:
The action is a sentence which remains the same throughout the round, e.g. 'Can I have a drink please?' and the adverbs reflect how an utterance may be said, e.g. 'loudly', 'shyly', 'sweetly', 'grumpily', 'angrily'.

Notes
- Teachers will need to adapt the vocabulary used in the adverb cue cards to match the language levels of the group.

- The children may need help with reading the cue cards.

Games

VERBAL SKILLS
I CAN APOLOGISE
Sorry
Ladders

SORRY

Key Skill
I can apologise

Cross Reference
I can say what I like and don't like

Other Skills
I can take turns
I can win or lose

Materials
A 'Snakes and Ladders' grid board with crosses marked on it to indicate a forfeit
A dice
A set of cards depicting situations when you need to say sorry (see Appendix B, p. 106)

How to Play
1. Play as you would for an ordinary game of 'Snakes and Ladders'. Each child takes it in turns to throw a dice and move along.

2. If a child lands on a 'cross' square they must pick up a 'sorry' card. The teacher helps with the reading and the child has to act out saying sorry.

Adaptations
To extend:
The children could miss a turn if they are unable to give an apology.

The other children have to vote on whether or not it was an acceptable and appropriate apology.

Note
It might be helpful to brainstorm when it is necessary to apologise before you start the game.

LADDERS

Key Skill
I can apologise

Cross Reference
I can show awareness of others

Other Skills
I can take turns
I can win or lose

Materials
None needed

How to Play
1. Explain how to play the game.

2. The children sit in two rows facing each other, legs in the middle, making a ladder.

3. The game is a race between two teams; care and speed are needed.

4. The person at the top of the 'ladder' on each side is the leader.

5. The leaders get up, run down the outside of the ladder, and come back up the middle, stepping over the children's legs.

6. The children run as fast as they can, but if they step on anyone they have to stop and say 'sorry (the person's name)'.

7. When the leaders get to the top, the next children go up the middle, down the outsides and back up the middle to their place.

8. The winning team is the one to get everyone back in their place.

Adaptations
To extend:
If the person forgets to say sorry, they have to go back and start again. The teacher and another child act as referees, one for each team.

Notes
•   Discuss why you say 'sorry' before the game begins.

•   Talk about other situations when you might accidentally hurt someone.

Appendix A

Ideas for 'Hello and goodbye' (see p. 72)

Scenarios

Having a party	Wanting help	Calling round to play
Borrowing something	Offering an outing	Telling about an accident
In a small shop	Getting into a taxi	Getting on to a bus
At the library	Interrupting someone	Meeting someone new
Taking a message	Meeting someone you haven't seen for a long time	Wanting to join in a game
Buying a ticket e.g. at the cinema	Thanking someone on the phone for a present	

Appendix B)

Ideas for 'Sorry' (see p. 103)

Sorry situations

1. You broke a friend's toy.
2. You kicked a ball through a window.
3. You drank a friend's juice.
4. You borrowed something and didn't return it.
5. You go away and Mum forgets to take your favourite toy. What does she say to you?
6. You spill your drink on the carpet.
7. You forget to brush your teeth.
8. You forget to bring your reading book back to school.
9. A friend has their bike stolen.
10. A friend breaks their arm.
11. A friend loses their cat.
12. A friend loses their favourite toy.
13. You say something horrible to a friend and upset them.
14. You hit somebody and make them cry.
15. You accidentally close the door on somebody and trap their fingers.
16. You are rude to somebody and they say, 'That was really unkind.'
17. You accidentally bump into somebody in the playground.
18. You tear your clothes at school. What do you say to your mum or dad?
19. You accidentally take home somebody else's towel after swimming.
20. You take the last piece of cake at dinner time, and the person behind you really wanted it.

Alphabetical Index of Games